# The Last Unkillable Thing

# The Last Unkillable Thing

\* \* \* \*

POEMS BY
*Emily Pittinos*

UNIVERSITY OF IOWA PRESS, *Iowa City*

University of Iowa Press, Iowa City 52242
Copyright © 2021 by Emily Pittinos
uipress.uiowa.edu
Printed in the United States of America

Cover design by TG Design
Art used on cover by Gabriela Holzer, www.gabrielahozer.com
Text design by Barbara Haines

Printed on acid-free paper

Library of Congress Cataloging-in-Publication Data

Names: Pittinos, Emily, author.
Title: The Last Unkillable Thing / Emily Pittinos.
Description: Iowa City: University of Iowa Press, [2021] | Series: Iowa
    Poetry Prize
Identifiers: LCCN 2020039786 (print) | LCCN 2020039787 (ebook) | ISBN
    9781609387648 (paperback) | ISBN 9781609387655 (ebook)
Subjects: LCGFT: Poetry.
Classification: LCC PS3616.I8848 L37 2021 (print) | LCC PS3616.I8848
    (ebook) | DDC 811/.6—dc23
LC record available at https://lccn.loc.gov/2020039786
LC ebook record available at https://lccn.loc.gov/2020039787

*for my father (1962–2014)*

*for my mother (1963–    )*

•

# CONTENTS

\* \* \* \*

# The Last Unkillable Thing

# Assuming, once again, it's done with

it's easy to think, *what's left,*
*now that I no longer*
*cower in the light of you—*

           A lapse in grief
is another emptiness; a space, in turn, filled
by the usual remembering: the unthinkable
made so possible as to become fact—*he vanished*
                             *and she went on—*

In my periphery,
every shadow is a new dead thing—

           the coyote dead beside the water, its clean bone
           the unwasting work of birds.

# Usual Ghosts

will they survive : the sparrows diving : I'm afraid to see
my lethal ways : my being : how

                         can anything die on such a day :

endless wheat : haloed
angels : I've never called upon

the fields of sun : the field of iris : tangible

                              rainbow : farmable rapture :

chicory tickles the roadside—soon my jar will be its jail—

finches, alive : flitting by in the color of corn : jay :
steel blue born soft : so soft as to seem forgivable : I

                    can't go long without
                    asking : beauty, its purpose :

                              to heal : how can anything : the sparrows :

the unwitting path : my reckless : the road
made endless by dark at my back : my insides

                         still and yet working : yellow bird a flurry in a ball jar : how

can anyone : the golden hour not an hour at all :

                    the brief imagining : the wreck undone :
                    to radiate as sun, forgiven : to be

## After

She replants hydrangeas beside the herb garden growing wild
with chive. Years ago, she hoped        for a simple spring
and cried when snow covered                her first daffodil.
I didn't expect           such sweet feeling; I should've known
her better then. Through the night      she stretches and stretches
his sweater across her chest. She says            she is nineteen
and lost all              over again. She says she'll stay alone
forever. I sing, *my mother*        *is not always my mother*. I say it
over and over again.

✳

*my mother is not always my mother most nights my father's widow knee-deep in ash garden I watch*

*my mother in knots always holding herself hostage with ice cube tray and faint smell in sweater*

*my mother now waiting thirty years to die told me so as we drove through a blown-open mountain mouth*

✳

They were deer     made still by signs of danger.     It may
take thirty years, or     she could go sooner.     With tight
lips they sipped red wine—my mother, my father's sisters
silently searching     for what they still had     in common.
They were desperate     to laugh. They drafted
paperwork; they said *sign here     and here*. They asked
would I want my sibling     if more tragedy came. I never
answered.     Each call could be the call     or the call
could never come.

✳

*the call to lift these hollow hackles this life hacked open cobbled out of my mind with worry I wait*

*the call to orphan me where would we how could we live I cannot be mother of lunches sex talk stay in school*

*the calling to transplant this one not my own this one my only one left to love is left*

✷

All night, I boil bones into broth for my only        sibling, who
has so few loved ones      left to hold them. I strain       the broth
through white cloth, wring it clean.         Always, more hunger
will come. Someday, I will become their mother.        I am
already their father. Most nights,       they lie beside our mother,
who rises without        needing to wake and grips the steering
wheel before dawn, dark dirt roads stretched        into an endless
onward. This is how we beat            the turning of the sun. I
hold my ear to the wall, hear time coming.

✴

*put my ear to hunger the earliest emptiness made room for others in this room I made by*

*putting my ear to the toppling tower of won't of can't of these extinguished blessings for which it's too late to*

*put my ear to the humming body of a bird held midair by instinct by simple breath*

✳

The Latest Tornado

But what of the wood duck, displaced, alone in a shadow?
        Its aimless waddle reminds: I have not yet
dragged myself back to who mothered me,
                the widow I ignore.

She, like me, fears the nothing left—
            the said, the unsaid. I sense
permanence brewing and go on

                dozing under dogwood. I collect
snapped branches, the blossoms hardly bruised—
        these I receive for my ambling, though I am
unworthy, the runaway
                daughter bowed by any storm.

## Wanting a Child

This condition is not like hoarding for winter.
     There may be no torpor here,
               no feast, either.

I see a fox, petrified in bog water.
     I envy the gall wasp, its egg
              a pincushion on the oak leaf.

This disruption will likely stay
           unnamed. I call it
    faceful of dove. I call it
    glass-choked gladiola. I know
    too little of life. I forget disappointment
              is a deft teacher.

On my hammock of barbed wire and chicken bone, I let
    my lamb's ear wither in the heat.

## Edge of Ruin

       The finest frost is torture—winter refusing
to roll over, an entire field of blight. The apple,
in fact, unbruisable—no burst blood in an orchard,
just dust
          rising from drops—but fragile
as you are, blight
a hundred ways:
                 what frost does
to the blossoms, what the cattail endures—
its explosion each autumn, its future
airborne. Seed lines the nest of my dread—

          forgive me; I don't wish even myself on you.

With Key in the Door

it is impossible to quit :

forecasting an alternate life : hazy glow in which
I am brighter : kinder : unorphanable : longing

is the undertow : I know living things do their best
to keep from dying : but what of the soft fox

always sprinting ahead of the pack : I set a trap
for what is good : I know the cantaloupe is ripe

when I smell sweetness through the skin : I imagine
the touch of joy : is unmistakable :

the belly of a bridegroom : the oyster
even without pearl : what happens when death

empties into the body : trap set and left : I return
to the lights off : I steady to bear : the too bitter

## After

It's too late      for questions like, *why this*      *woman*
*to whom care didn't come.*   I should know better      by now.
My father's widow says, *please, stop,*          *we have enough*
*to worry about without*          *your fear*—mortgage, secret
loans, the roof      frozen      warped      spits
as the family goes on          shrinking—his mother, her
father. It is simple for          the hurt. It snags in tall
dead grasses,      becomes light itself.      It sways.

*

*snags in tall debts owed to car roof guitar widow's thigh grabbed by the lake trout trapped barehanded*

*snags in fall red won't drop how loved ones become squires of together become drunk on it helps it doesn't I'm*

*snagged by all dead nets of what if or not if but who will tumble next through a tomb of tall tales slow fading forever*

✳

I've mapped myself          in the house of women
flitting from room to room          in his pilled flannel shirts.
They collapse      into his absence. They tell          his tales.
My world          swallows itself.          Did he leave his life
to me?      I go on a trip. I go          on another. I take a lover
and then another. I see          the plain hold light against
its chest; the ocean          rolls in fits of laughter. Always,
a thin hum of guilt for the ones I left, but          shrinking
all the time.

✳

*thin hum of woman on the lam for slaughter house mortared by morbid year of wondering when why*

*this sum leaves me liable for women left to pierce themselves on goodbye shrapnel*

*thin thrum rich with regret ears pricked to predict what stalks us next growing wild in the wings*

✳

## I Grow Less Visible

It wasn't the sense but how it came—the light behind
the banister, splinters aglow.
                              A silhouette can sway
a person—the woman releasing
        her bra behind scrim. My breath more alive
than when held in.


                    I'm not as soft as I look.
There was grit before grief took me.
            To some lucidity is fleeting. Screen door
barely torn. I can't help
                        but compare this to what came
before: happy once, a notion that torments


no matter the reality. Light
                        so bright it can deter
thievery. Undone, undoing,
                        undo. The evening
sucking grapes down to skins. Skin:
        the scrim that keeps the body in. Leg hair
illuminated. In this mind, I can't be sure

of where I came from,

or if I ever was. Rust between

the lips. The moment

teaches, but I live behind, ahead. I will

never be power. I can say ghost

until I scream. Little death. A stranger

may see my sex from here. Flare


between the knees. Muscle

too easily manipulated. If I take another moment

to appease,

I'm over. I can't

not be bothered: the neat waist, the smallest

tasks. I fold the cloth

I call skin. This I wore


to the end of the world. As if worry

were not worthless. I empty

pockets, toss coins in a drawer.

Doesn't it hurt

to be human. I'm so human I could die.

## It Is Not Animal to Forgive

To have been held by the most unkind lovers—or
not held, exactly, but held down,

                                    however gently, my mind
twisting every gesture into tenderness. Perhaps

this is why I hold pleasure, now, at a distance.
You can admire the untouched forever
and never hurt, or at least not as much. The ivy lush,
lovely no matter how poisonous.

                                    I'd imagine bucks
scraping bark from sugar maple, lonely
for does bedded down in black raspberry.
Who was the doe here, the thorn, the wick of green—

It's a shame, the shame I felt. All that time
transforming myself into something
more lovable. It aches

                        to admit all I wanted. Mine
may be a greedy way of being,
or naïve enough to be quaint. The buck
content before the final shot.

A man dresses a deer—quick split, blood
guttered by rainfall—before pressing a woman
to his own soft belly. To be
so unsorry, so unbound. Am I, too,
at fault—

## Trembling on the Skin of a Droplet

Frost softens into steam that spills off the morning,
and at the tip of each blade, a diamond quivers.
I am as susceptible to beauty as I am any other pain.
The pang of clouds dulling, and then the rain
obliterated to mist by the wind.
                                    Water in the air
can grey distance—that ghost of an egret poised at the lip
of the pond—but then, the grass dry and ordinary by noon.
How much awe have I missed by looking away?
How much pain?
                    I turn to you without remembering
what we decided in the end, whether to keep our distance,
or to close it. As the outer wonders shift—
awe into threat
                    into the threat grown tiresome—
desire returns. This poor, dumb animal,
see her light out into the day,
both after prey, and as.

## All in Dissolve

A ringing, not in the ear, but in the mind—
cotton-headed confusion of day breaking
under the weight of a sudden noon. Through the night

dream worked as a woodchipper, tearing the unwanted
into manageable parts: *perhaps it was you*
                                    *who bore down*
*on care until it shredded; you, nuzzling, who let need pose*
*as affection.* Icicles slough off

the roof in glassy blasts. From the window: the coyote
romps across the frozen lake, tosses snow up,
chomps down, a game
                          he plays on the grave of an elk,
which you, naked in bed, once watched
fall through the ice and drown.

## I Remember How Cold I Will Be

Following the snow depressed by some strange foot, following some
  strange strain against love left, for now, in the yellow house,

I step over the seed released from its spine and the winter's hardened
  slipper beside a gravel pit. Lately, a habit

of thirst in the night. I wake with it, and do nothing, my body a tumble-
  weed beside another—toward, and away, and toward.

We each accept what little comfort the other can afford. What little I can
  accept. Yes, sure. I've suffered. Is this more?

How basic I become in my brooding, how racked with ho-hum in some
  noon hours. Meanwhile: the lavender sigh

of riverside flora. The river's reflection snaps into a rushing sky. How
  many chances have I missed to force

the thaw that always burns, though for the better, for a time? The poison
  sumac makes a puff of its one branch. Snow

outlines this moonscape, the moss, the lake, the lichen now a jewel
  gleaming under powdery teeth. Funny, how elk have feet; funny,

how they are nearby but unseen. What is barren to one is shelter to
   another. Is this suffering? I am famished. Is that?

Even the goose, pausing at these banks on its way elsewhere, plucks
   morsels from river muck—its beak glistening, onyx.

Should I, too, leave, in order to return? Yellow light on the yellow house.
   Who else could be here to notice you, to notice being here?

## In Wolf's Clothing

This butter-colored dress may not be enough—satin, chiffon, cinch
the body in an hourglass. Craving keeps like the stench
of stoker coal in a pheasant-feather crown, and from each
sneezy clump of goldenrod leaps

a new vise of what-if and to think,

*I once wanted what I have.*

I've had more; I've had less; I embarrass myself.

I hunt for a necktie, copperhead in the stampede of suits—
all along a plum rolling like a thumb in my mouth—or sequin boots
to dance diamonds on my atrium floor, the horsehair plaster
cracked and crumbled there. The dust of it.
One thread will tug the body bare. I tug, and mend; I mend.

I can't be helped.

## Loss Becomes Me

I fold into topsoil with eggshell, banana peel, rabbit shit. The slow dissolve will leave richness, I am told. The garden will grow back fuller—heavy bend at the neck.

The moringa leaf pinned to my curtain sprouts roots around its rim. This, my best attempt at necromancy, impotent though it is.

The perennial threat is pleasure, its potential to rush in along with all I have shaken. Curse cyclical craving:

*but hadn't I*
*the shattered evergreen—hadn't I*
*the wintered bone—*

The blue jay, nest robber by nature, is too animal to feel shame for the dead it makes. I can't keep myself from apology. All the minutiae gone unforgiven.

*forgive my wilting*
*basil—forgive pillow slick*
*with sniffle, with wept—*

I kill the clover taking root on  my  sill,
harmless but uninvited. The grit of another
the other threat.

Spores invade, ascend as the golden hour
leaves a trellis of ivy angelic. Or is it apt
for capturing? A golden net of leaves, or
a glowing brood of wings?

Pleasures I do not fear: the orange peeled
in its continuous coil, cedar insular in snow.
The rest is the rest.

Torment is the weed I cultivate best.

*hadn't I*
*the unhung suet—hadn't I*
*the fled red room—*

Through the dim pane, *never enough*
pours in so easily. Dead basil. Always
the issue of light.

.

# The Days Shorter, and Yet

When the red bird strikes the window, it is me
who takes blame. I do
                        the autopsy, yank
rough stones from the throat, clay widow
from the heart.
                        I treat my flesh as clay
for sculpt and smash—red welt of snapped elastic,
red cage for blooming
                        tumor. I grow uglier
by the day—the truth: I contain a destroyer. Tensions
eased by snifters of toxin; another
succulent to replace the last
                        "unkillable" thing. I scrub
the daikon pale, smooth the carrot gnarled
by wax paper earth—barrier to perfection,
barrier to any elsehood.
                        My mortal *no, please, look away.*

✳ ✳ ✳

## She Must Have a Bit of Green to Look At

She steps into the wool of midnight,
her life a line of tin cups
put to the lips of others:

      pale pale skin,
      straw hair overgrown,

      her crumbled well of caring for.

She would take a bullet train through plains
      into daydreams of whole
      oranges, bitter grape seeds
      spat past snow.

Against the telephone booth, she taps
her red ember,
        smoke ring: a blast of blue tinsel.

✳

In the night hall she rises, razes

a vase to the floor. She leaves it:
the glass unable
to glitter its warning
in the humless dark.

In the morning: mice
casually rinsing
their puny hands in a puddle.

*Even they*, she thinks, *cower not from me.*

✳

She no longer has room for the menagerie inside her;

its upkeep taxes her every resource—the falcon
demands more quail than she can catch; the lion

roars doubt throughout her; the boa
constricts—it is all he knows.

Could her beasts be forever

imprisoned in amber.

Could she extract the clamor from her heart cage,
wing by wing, limb by limb.

✳

She pierces the dead center
of every flower with wire, knots nets
in the hopes of catching her saddest self unawares.

It is not revenge she seeks but confrontation.
*Why must you torture me . . .*

She will smack her own answer out,
if she must.

*

Instead, she summons
tins overflowing with sea-
glass, the rustle-clink-clink of plunging
her hands through an offering of bits.

Each is a survivor of treatment
tougher than her own—the promise

that rough and tumble may amount
to smooth, cool being.

✳

She captures a recluse in her bordeaux glass,
the bulb's slope an insurmountable trap
slippery as blackest ice—film of danger

on a county road, the many cars
she saw careen, the several in which
she rode down slopes of her own dark promise
only to be saved

                by what, exactly—milliseconds,
reflexive belt, bush that volunteered itself
for sprouting decades prior, a simple
seed in the breeze.

＊

She hears the winter cardinal called
*the rust-red of a barn.* Where and when
barns became red, she cannot say.
The barns she knows
are weathered to splinters at the roadside,
silver-grey

        of old wood gone unpainted,
nearly glinting at twilight
as she bucks down dirt roads,
the wildflowers a tickle at the shoulder,
the nodding cornflower
still blue, not captured, not yet

the colorless ghost
at her bedside by morning.

✳

It takes focus to flood herself serene.
She lets the sea into the room:

the tide spoils the wallpaper;
an urchin sticks in the shag.

She lounges on the coral armchair, rough
to touch—
          *I won't be what gets me—*
the brush fire now a fizzle between her legs.

✳

She hates them: the creatures
that burst unbidden into her line
of questioning.

             She parks her self
beside a crop of mosaic corn.

One shucked husk reveals true gold,
another the hide of a hare.

She strokes the fur against her cheek—
        *when else has such tenderness—*

She rests in the plot of stalks.

             A fog of butterflies surprises,
             kaleidoscope airborne.

✳✳✳✳

## Hot Spring:

ankle-deep : riverbed of rose : quartz caught :
pool of heat : earth a furnace :   subcutaneous
molten shift  :  I finger the rock's pelt of algae :
geode    entombed    by   bloom   :    to think   :
not long ago : I wanted to kill my loneliness :
downstream  :   a heron drying its wings  :  mites
dying there :  to think  :   sunlight a killer too :
a person  can  get  used to anything

# After

I am no less wild, no less     stalked. Before sleep in a grove,
I seek peace. I see her trip through the mess          of brambles,
her white night-         gown, torn        by thorns. I see the long
fall to her knees. Why                 must the mind make burrs of its
unrest? It was my job          to chop her hair        shocked white
by trauma. I'd scatter            the trimmings as others do ashes.
Useless task—not even a bird would build a home of such fear.

# Study of a Lone Beast

The false widow builds her web
in a chasm—the grace of risk,
her passage of silk an act
of survival.
            The last moment
I gave myself up, I cannot say.

This is how I find my mind
must not belong to me at all:

without caution, my illness
may tumble in—avalanche
all morning and into the night.

Suppose the worst does happen—
        by sunrise the web wrecked, glittering
        with snowfall, and where has she gone,
        the queen of this realm?

## Subnivean *(or Holding Back the Year)*


I expected the snow, but waking stuns.
A world of storm struck white—distance
collapsed by an absence of shadow, the valley
either acre or infinite. I must become so still
to hear: a rustle, a hum

                    that sounds human, though
it couldn't be. Not here. I never meant
to be this lonely. Coated saplings, nearly invisible—
they, too, become what they carry.


✳

Once, hemmed in by a blizzard,
I boiled snow to drink. I clutched
a pillowcase of pet snakes to my belly.
They'd have died without my human heat;
they are the only ones.
                              Now, a scarf of breath.
The slinking creature barely glimpsed.
Bark once marked by velvety antlers—
the newly budded made sharp by attack.
The deer only multiply, though I hear
they are starving each other to death.
I've heard a snowstorm is only good
for the path one can leave. Even sparrows flee
the ice hour. Now my way is the only way home.

*

I'd be lost

       without my own bright footpath: tilled snow:
cloud cover: moonglow refracted: the shotgun crack
of a bough unburdened.

                Could I walk off the hours
I've spent ashamed, attempting a life
that would make the dead proud?
What would it look like,
how much would it weigh?

✳

In the hall of iced cedars, it seems possible
to forget the spring. Forgotten: the lilac bush
that leans over the water, a *widowmaker*.
Forgotten: honeysuckles that carry on
with their wafting, the dew I received
as a blessing. Spring
                          is only a spasm—
before long, the weeping cherry's hem of petals
fallen to nourish the earth.
Winter is what endures, the crystal casket
it grows around the world.

✳

There—a gunshot, just a disturbance
through the trees—far off, an uncertain kill.
How awful, death relived at its slightest suggestion:
the trail a smooth passing, but then
the fallen animal.
                    A corpse is a corpse,
that way I did not see him—cold,
and colder. I've become
                    the one to cry *adore me*
in the direction of all there is,
the nearest flock startled into separate explosions.
It is always the birds who fall back together,
leaving the silence to roost.

※

How long have I followed tracks without realizing
everything stalks all else?
                              Animals, exposed, don't know
harmlessness. This land without mercy.
This whipping drift so dense
it may as well be the blizzard that blew me here.
There are kingdoms under snowpack, tunnels
unseen unless destroyed.
                              The knot of mice
breathes heat into the haven. A fox
listens for its kill before tearing into the snow.

✳

Winter rain arrives, pocks snowbanks, exposes
deer tracks, their piss. The holes left by hooves
are deep, flooded with bog water, its frozen mosses.
The river high and fast. Dead grasses,
cedar fronds dipped into water like wicks into wax—
bright bulbs of ice
                    I want to shatter. How much
of enjoying a place is destroying it? Marks made,
however unlasting, lasting. I've killed a creature
to see if I could. I can't tame myself.
Or won't. I flick snow from my jean cuff.
I could stuff a songbird into my mouth.

✳

Once, I found a finch's skeleton still
hanging from a glue trap. The dead
do not speak, to me
they've said all they can. Hours spent
ashamed, attempting. What will be possible
when I'm no longer sorry? I can want
until I'm blue. Blue dark cast on snow, the burn
of fingers coming, once again,
alive.
      In this mind, I may trudge
toward the ravine of forgetting—
a stampede of velvet horses,
a dream too new to burn.

✳

Forgotten: the giddy
sunflower field, the frog spared
beside the river. Encased in winter,
all too clear: a gasping body glows,
a moon sinks on the end of a wire.
I've come a long way
to do my goodbyeing.

What will it look like?

How much will it weigh?

✳

During grey days, I grew
more afraid. I feared even the fear,
the staying afraid.
                    Why is it gloom
produces the most angelic light,
days cast as more precious
in shades of platinum, the branches
locking horns again, birch skin silver
as scrim? More awful still
to find this way of being is bearable,
if only that.
                    In our garden, autumn stalks
of daffodils were braided before their freeze
and decay. Imagine,
all the long-awaited releases.

✳

Movement in the thaw. Warmth
of movement without touch. There: a deer gone still
beside the river. The iridescent eyes. The moment
before she leaves me. Light snags
in the rain, threads of light. I hear lightning
can spring from heat alone. But not here,
in the land of aurora, blush of green
across the cloudless sky.
What follows?
                    Sweet water
flowing down the bend. Sweetness made bitter
by its passing. Made sweeter. Made. All of this
made. A path long eroded made longer.

## I Would Let Go, If Only It Came Naturally

The water has a way of happening, lapping at Mosquito Beach, wearing
        the sandstone down sweetly, layer by layer.

I can feel it coming on, my season of lavish suffering, the *why me why me*
        *why me why me* that leaves me snowblind in the asking.

Pennies planted to coax hydrangeas produced a crocus by mistake,
        its beak opening through spring snow.

I begged for rain instead (knowing the late-late frost is a kind of murder),
        so feel failed prayer hot against my ear. It is terribly easy

to take on another's pain. Or at least to consider it taken. My eye
        shimmers with robbery. Should I be ashamed?

I may say the wrong things, but there is no right way to say nothing
        will change. On my dulled day, the poet dares to brag

he could break into blossom. What do lost daughters burst into?

## Torpor, Interrupted

The cold snap at last releases
the ginkgo leaves, the ground gold,
       and before long: it is going
to snow—breath seen
                escaping, hot.


Glare-white noon dims
to blue-black. Another fantasy
about the vessels flirtation can open.
I am too alone
          to sleep, too aware
      of the burden absence brings, or perhaps
too unaccustomed to peace.


        Nightjars bed down in snow, take flight
           at the first sight of danger;
I remember the nights when the danger
        was me—strange hackles, all pricked up.


I'm hungry again, reliving the latest commotion,
          the rules broken. This body
dragged around so the mind
could take part, decide
        what is alluring, worthy. The snow

is what does it to me, landscape a whetstone
     I slide against until I become
the animal. I am
         not actually out for blood, just want
       the feel of it, loosed
           inside, its vision: *I'll have. I'll be had.*

# NOTES and ACKNOWLEDGMENTS

Grateful acknowledgments to the editors and readers of the following publications for their generous gifts of time and attention, and for giving many of these poems their first appearances: the *Adroit Journal* ("I Would Let Go, If Only It Came Naturally"), *Beloit Poetry Journal* ("Assuming, once again, it's done with," "Subnivean [*or Holding Back the Year*]," "Torpor, Interrupted"), *Denver Quarterly* ("It Is Not Animal to Forgive"), the *Laurel Review* ("With Key in the Door" [first published as "Answers"]), *Michigan Quarterly Review* ("Trembling on the Skin of a Droplet"), *Mississippi Review* ("Loss Becomes Me," "In Wolf's Clothing"), *Moss* ("The Latest Tornado"), *Nat. Brut* ("The Days Shorter, and Yet"), *Ploughshares* ("Wanting a Child"), *Third Coast Magazine* ("I Grow Less Visible"), *Tupelo Quarterly* ("Hot Spring:").

"She Must Have a Bit of Green to Look At" borrows its title from language in Virginia Woolf's "Street Haunting." "I Remember How Cold I Will Be" borrows its title from the final line of Lucie Brock-Broido's "Carrowmore." "Wanting a Child" is inspired by a poem of the same name by Jorie Graham. "I Would Let Go, If Only It Came Naturally" refers to "A Blessing" by James Wright.

There are many brilliant and caring people behind these poems, especially since this is my first book and has therefore taken a life up until now to make. Please know that if you have been a teacher, mentor, family member, or friend to me, you are remembered and admired, and I am grateful.

Thank you to Brenda Shaughnessy and everyone at the University of Iowa Press for believing in this work and giving this book a future.

Thank you to my Interlochen teachers in the fly-fishing school of poetry: Jack Driscoll, Michael Delp, Anne-Marie Oomen, Mika Perrine, Katey Schultz. Thank you to my University of Michigan mentors and family: Keith Taylor, A. Van Jordan, Laura Kasischke, Conor Anderson, Ian Klipa, Rowan Niemisto, Kayla Upadhyaya, Hayley Hershman. Thank you to the Bucknell poets who met and saw me through a time of tremendous grief: K. A. Hays, Deirdre O'Connor, Justin Boening, Carolina Ebeid, Diana Khoi Nguyen. Thank you to my first students, my colleagues, and my professors at Washington University in St. Louis, including Carl Phillips, Mary Jo Bang, Kathleen Finneran, Edward McPherson, and the cohorts concurrent, above, and below who poked at early drafts of the poems here. A special thank you to those who read this manuscript in its entirety, often more than once, and informed its shape: Eric Stiefel, Serena Solin, Luther Hughes, Gabrielle Bates, Bailey Spencer, Claire Askew, Caroline Kessler. Thank you to my beloved family: Mom & Jamie, the Pittinoses, the Lipsons, the Canters, Aaron & Townes. And thank you to those without category: Gabriela Holzer, Kerri Webster, Catie Young, Paul Tran, Carlene Kucharczyk, Sarah Audsley, Sebastian Matthews, Chen Peng, Amy Sailer, Kelly Caldwell, Duncan Sprattmoran, Sarah Jane Johnson, Jamie Delp, Joyce Harrington Bahle, Jim Harrison, Dan Beachy-Quick, Cole Swensen, Srikanth Reddy, Erin Belieu, francine j. harris, Andrea Beauchamp.

I am also grateful to the following organizations whose support, given in the forms of time, funding, and community, made this work possible: the Bucknell Seminar for Undergraduate Poets, the Hopwood Program at the University of Michigan, the Crosshatch Hill House Program, the YoungArts Foundation, Vermont Studio Center, and Washington University in St. Louis.

# IOWA POETRY PRIZE AND
## EDWIN FORD PIPER POETRY AWARD WINNERS

1987

Elton Glaser,
*Tropical Depressions*
Michael Pettit, *Cardinal Points*

1988

Bill Knott, *Outremer*
Mary Ruefle, *The Adamant*

1989

Conrad Hilberry,
*Sorting the Smoke*
Terese Svoboda,
*Laughing Africa*

1990

Philip Dacey, *Night Shift*
*at the Crucifix Factory*
Lynda Hull, *Star Ledger*

1991

Greg Pape, *Sunflower*
*Facing the Sun*
Walter Pavlich, *Running near the*
*End of the World*

1992

Lola Haskins, *Hunger*
Katherine Soniat,
*A Shared Life*

1993

Tom Andrews,
*The Hemophiliac's Motorcycle*
Michael Heffernan,
*Love's Answer*
John Wood, *In Primary Light*

1994

James McKean, *Tree of Heaven*
Bin Ramke, *Massacre of*
*the Innocents*
Ed Roberson, *Voices Cast Out to*
*Talk Us In*

1995

Ralph Burns, *Swamp Candles*
Maureen Seaton,
*Furious Cooking*

1996

Pamela Alexander, *Inland*
Gary Gildner, *The Bunker*
*in the Parsley Fields*
John Wood, *The Gates of*
*the Elect Kingdom*

1997
  Brendan Galvin,
  *Hotel Malabar*
1997
  Leslie Ullman,
  *Slow Work through Sand*

1998
  Kathleen Peirce,
  *The Oval Hour*
  Bin Ramke, *Wake*
  Cole Swensen, *Try*

1999
  Larissa Szporluk, *Isolato*
  Liz Waldner, *A Point Is
  That Which Has No Part*

2000
  Mary Leader,
  *The Penultimate Suitor*

2001
  Joanna Goodman,
  *Trace of One*
  Karen Volkman, *Spar*

2002
  Lesle Lewis, *Small Boat*
  Peter Jay Shippy,
  *Thieves' Latin*

2003
  Michele Glazer,
  *Aggregate of Disturbances*
  Dainis Hazners,
  *(some of) The Adventures of
  Carlyle, My Imaginary Friend*

2004
  Megan Johnson, *The Waiting*
  Susan Wheeler, *Ledger*

2005
  Emily Rosko,
  *Raw Goods Inventory*
  Joshua Marie Wilkinson,
  *Lug Your Careless Body
  out of the Careful Dusk*

2006
  Elizabeth Hughey, *Sunday Houses
  the Sunday House*
  Sarah Vap, *American Spikenard*

2008
  Andrew Michael Roberts,
  *something has to happen next*
  Zach Savich,
  *Full Catastrophe Living*

2009
  Samuel Amadon, *Like a Sea*
  Molly Brodak,
  *A Little Middle of the Night*